MY FRIEND CONSIDER

Reflections on Life, Love, Courage
and Your Eternal Soul

DRU ANN KENNER

SECOND EDITION

ISBN: 979-8-9942694-04

Table of Contents

My Friend Consider...

By Dru Ann Kenner

A Few Words about Dru Ann – the Amazing Woman We Called Mom

Before you read her words, allow us to introduce the woman who wrote them. She was not famous or widely known, but she shaped our lives in ways no biography could fully capture. We simply knew her as Mom.

Our mother, Dru Ann, was born on May 28, 1929. Her childhood unfolded in the hard years between the Great Depression and World War ll. Shaped by those early years, she developed a gentle resilience that she would later share with us. Love, compassion, honesty, and innocence were her calling cards. She would often say "Thank you, kind sir" as her expression of gratitude, and if the words did not come, you could see it in her eyes. Our mother was a happy person. She worked constantly to make ends meet but remained almost penniless. Timid and subservient, yet somehow deeply generous. She looked for the good in every situation and rarely complained. That was Mom.

Courage was not something you would expect from such a delicate soul. Yet courage is what it took for our Mother to separate herself from a relationship that had become unbearable. Married at 23, she spent the next 22 years as a dutiful wife and loving mother—living with a fear that only grew over time. By the early 1970s, at the height of her emotional desperation, she began receiving gentle, comforting affirmations that rose into her consciousness. She carefully transcribed those messages into a journal. This book, and the two that followed, emerged from that extraordinary communication.

First published in 1984, this second edition of MY FRIEND CONSIDER preserves the text as it was originally presented to the public. Its Early Modern English style—reminiscent of the

Shakespearean era—is filled with "thees" and "thous." Two companion books, MY FRIEND CONSIDER THAT WHICH IS and MY FRIEND CONSIDER THAT WHICH SHALL BE, also transcribed in the early 1970s, use plain English and reflect the writing conventions of their time, including the generic use of masculine pronouns. The intention was not to exclude any gender but simply to follow the linguistic norms of that era.

A preview of the book MY FRIEND CONSIDER THAT WHICH IS can be found at the end of this book—worth a read before its full release in 2026.

We share this remembrance as her children, with love for the woman who shaped our lives and whose words now continue on their own journey.

—Daniel and Cynthia Kenner

A word about the Journal Pages

Following each writing, you will find two lined pages offered as a quiet space to reflect or to record your own thoughts, memories, questions, or insights that arise as you read. Whenever you feel drawn to pause and write, these pages will be waiting for you—whether days, months, or even years later. When the time feels right, they can become a place to capture how her words meet you in your own season of life.

Each upon earth at some point asks the four questions of life: WHO AM I? WHERE DID I COME FROM? WHY AM I HERE? AND WHERE AM I GOING?

There is a restless element within the self which ever states, "I must be eternal." Indeed, we are eternal beings, moving ever onward in the search for love, joy, and understanding.

Some upon earth have opened selves to receive from others further along the path and who, at present, are upon the unseen plane of vibrational existence.

Man calls this process automatic writing—it could more aptly be stated inter-spheric communication (IC).

In such manner were the writings contained in this short volume transferred from those in one realm to those upon earth.

Yours to enjoy and contemplate, my friend, and consider.

My Friend,
Consider Thy Name

My friend, consider thy name. At birth, a word was appointed unto thy form, and this word was thy name. Yes, my friend, in the beginning was the word.

At that moment, when the name was appointed unto thee, thou didst have several names besides, for thy name was 'son' and thy name was 'brother' and thy name was 'nephew' and 'grandson', and so, thou wert one and thou wert many, and these names were thine because of circumstance. And perhaps, circumstance added other names to thee—'husband', 'father', 'uncle', 'grandfather'—this is all as it should be, for this is the way of life.

In the path of years which thou hast traveled in the earth, thou hast added unto thyself names untold, for thy name has been 'doctor', 'shopkeeper', 'chimneysweep', 'charlatan'; thy name has been saint, and thy name has been sinner. Thou hast stated, "I am happy," and thy name was 'happy'; thou hast said, "I am tired," and thy name was 'tired'; and as many times as thou hast stated, "I AM" thy name has differed–albeit in repetition.

As many times of the moment that thou hast stated, "I AM," thou hast repeated the very words of God, for he said, "I AM that I AM." Thou choosest by thy thought what thy name shall be, but in thy alwaysness, my friend, remember this–the first of the names appointed unto thee was a word, and in the beginning was the word, and the word was with God.

Reflections

_____

_____

_____

_____

_____

_____

_____

_____

_____

_____

_____

_____

_____

_____

_____

_____

_____

_____

_____

_____

_____

My Friend, Consider Thy Savings

My friend, consider thy savings.

Thou dost surely have a storeroom in which thou hast accumulated trinkets and gifts and reminders of memories, and thou dost surely sift through them now and then, and thou sayest, "All this is mine, and all this is good, and I shall keep it." And thou dost surely have, buried in the ground, or locked in some banker's vault, coins and paper barter which thou hast accumulated, and thou sayest, "All this is mine, and all this is good, and I shall keep it." And thou dost surely have, in the rooms of thy house, all those things which thou hast accumulated for thy needs, and thou sayest, "All this is mine, and all this is good, and I shall keep it."

My friend, thou dost still have the unworn cloak in thy storeroom, and thou didst have it the day a stranger came to thy door in the rain and said, "Kind sir, a day's work I shall give thee in exchange for an old cloak to keep me warm against this dark and dreary sky." Thou sayest, "I'm sorry, my man, I have only the cloak upon mine own back," and thou didst send him away with thy lie.

Thou hast still many coins in the banker's vault, and thou didst have them there the day thy neighbor came to thee and said, "Could I but borrow twenty pieces of silver, my good friend—I will surely repay thee with my wages, and two silver coins in addition to the twenty." Thou sayest, "I'm sorry, my neighbor, but I have only enough coins to buy bread to put upon mine own table," and thou didst send him away with thy lie.

And thou hast still all those things in thy house that thou didst have the day the young widow came to thee and said, "Kind sir, I shall do thy washing for thee, and bake thy cakes, if thou wilt but give me a portion of flour to make bread for my two hungry children." And thou sayest, "Much is the pity, my fair young miss, for times are hard and my cupboards are bare," and thou didst send her away with thy lie.

Remember this, my friend, that when thy body is set into the ground, as some day it will be, thou shalt not take with thee thine accumulation in the storeroom, and thou shalt not take with thee thine accumulation of coins in the banker's vault, and thou shalt not take with thee thine accumulation of goods within the walls of thy house. And yet, as strange as it may be, thou wilt surely take with thee thine entire savings, thine accumulation of lies, and thy soul shall weep.

Reflections

MY FRIEND CONSIDER

My Friend,
Consider The Forest

My friend, consider the forest. Is it not haven and home to the creatures who scamper along its floor and make their nests and lairs amongst the tree trunks... Is it not a place of delight, where the ever-unfolding day casts its shadows, and life beneath its branches goes on much the same as yesterday and yesterday... Is it not a peaceful place, where the activities of itself are carried on in order and sameness—the squirrel gathers its cache for the winter which will come, and then the winter comes... Is it not a pleasant place to spend a day with thy neighbor, exploring its many trails and mysteries?

Ah yes, my friend, the forest is an awesome place... mighty, and set apart, and yet, at times it can become a desolate place if one wanders off alone and becomes unsure of the way to go. And it can become a place of panic and of desperation when one ventures farther and farther in endless circles.

My friend, are there not those among you who somehow, somewhere have wandered off from the ordered path of their minds and lives into strange and frightening trails of thought and happenings... those who have taken a wrong turn or ventured too far?

My friend, thou canst be certain that when word comes of one lost neighbor in the forest of a mountainside, men will gather together to hunt and to call... to follow trails and challenge time until the lost is found. Indeed, this is noble and majestic and is the way of godly men.

It is sad, my friend, that men cannot see as clearly the same lostness within the heart of his troubled neighbor, for it is likely that if he could see, he would gather together his own forces of love and compassion and bring the groping one once again to safety.

Reflections

_____

_____

_____

_____

_____

_____

_____

_____

_____

_____

_____

_____

_____

_____

_____

_____

_____

_____

_____

_____

_____

_____

My Friend,
Consider The Seed

My friend, consider the seed.

Surely, thou art a reasonable man and thou knowest these two truths. This... that the seed which is planted will grow. And this... that that which happeneth within the seed is not of thy doing, for thou art but the sower, the caretaker, the waterer of plants.

And if thou art a man of wisdom, my friend, thou canst envision the flower and the fruit which is certain to come forth, for a wise man is aware of the exactness of the Law of Growth. So too, thou must tend the soil of thine own being and plant therein the seeds of that which thou dost truly desire.

My friend, use caution, for it is true that that which is planted shall produce after its kind. Wouldst thou embed seeds of fear in the garden of thy soul? Lo, recall... that which I fear has come upon me. Or wouldst thou plant seeds of hatred and then glance about thee and cry... "By God and by heaven I am justified in my hatred... hear my story... now this... now that!"

Thou art but deceiving thyself, for if thou sowest seeds of fear, thou shalt dwell in the shadows, darting here and there to avoid even the beating of thine own heart, and if thou sowest seeds of hatred, thou shalt dwell in the rocky caverns of the earth where the thunder of thine own curses shall ever echo in thine ears.

By God and by heaven, the Law of Growth is the same for all, and thou canst not reverse it at any time. Thou hast but one recourse if thou dost not care to reap the harvest of that which thou hast planted and that is this... to quickly... with one stroke... plow under that which thou hast sown and replace it with other seed.

Reflections

_____

_____

_____

_____

_____

_____

_____

_____

_____

_____

_____

_____

_____

_____

_____

_____

_____

_____

_____

_____

My Friend,
Consider Lovesong

My friend, consider lovesong. Is
it not the melody which fills the
heart of only 'two' and transports them to distant shores of the universe... for truly, all the
whispers of the ages are ever the same flowing
tune of rapture and ecstasy.

"Beloved, know me... come to me... be
with me... be me... beloved, loving you is the
dove flying free upon the winds of time... it
is the brook tumbling down the hillside... it
is the evening afterglow and the pale velvet
of dawning skies. Beloved, loving you is the
uncovering of buried treasures long locked
within my soul... it is a reuniting with God from
whom I turned away long ago in my loneliness
and sorrow. Beloved, loving you is the forever

of yesterday and the forever of tomorrow, here with me in the moment of now. Beloved, thy voice is sweeter than all the songs that angels sing, for thou art the supreme singing angel and when thou art gone from me, if only for an hour, thy presence lingers... surrounding me with lovesong which beats with every beat of my heart... Is it possible, my beloved, that thou hast excited within me that which is holy... for has it not been said that God is love."

Oh yes, my friend, for a time, lovesong plays its rhapsody to each, and if thou art fortunate, thou wilt absorb it into thy being and let it ever echo in the chambers of thy heart.

Reflections

MY FRIEND CONSIDER

My Friend, Consider The Rainy Day

My friend, consider the rainy day. Ah, the showers welcomed by earth and all the growing things therein... the very life of stream and river and lake and plant and animal and man. Shalt thou not ever behold the rain in awesome wonder?

But what is this, my friend, this strangeness which thou hast appointed unto the rainy day? Thou hast declared it to be a time of sickness or of aged infirmity or of calamity or a time of lack. These are indeed, strange words which thou speakest... "I shall store it away for a rainy day"...

Dost thou not know what power thou art committing to thy fearful imaginings? Dost thou not know that thou shalt declare a thing and it shall be done unto thee as thou dost believe?

My friend, awaken quickly and see the rainy day as it truly is... a bestower of life and of health, of growth and of supply... quickly, my friend, before thine own rainy day of turmoil come tumbling down upon thy shoulders and surely drown thee.

And if thou thinkest to speak of the rainy day in jest, to be in tune with the utterances of thy neighbor, use caution, for in time, a man can become convinced by his oft spoken words. And thou wilt find, my friend, that it is also true that thou shalt give account for every idle word.

Reflections

_____

_____

_____

_____

_____

_____

_____

_____

_____

_____

_____

_____

_____

_____

_____

_____

_____

_____

_____

My Friend,
Consider Candles

My friend, consider candles.

Thee and thy neighbor have built towers in the sky, and in thy towers thou hast constructed a thousand and a thousand rooms, but tell me for a fact... dost thou light them with candles?

No? Oh, thou hast harnessed an unseen force and set it to do thy bidding and it is this that lights thy rooms. Is that not marvelous, my friend, wonderous indeed. Pray... what is this force which thou hast captured? Thou knowest not? Thou knowest only that it has a name and it performs according to thy wishes.

Pray... from thy great men of science, what say they? We have given it a name and it performs according to our directed desires, yet we know not what it is nor from whence it cometh.

My friend, is it not awesome that thee and thy neighbor have such faith in this unknown force that thou knowest to merely press a lever and the unseen will direct itself into that channel which will fulfill thy purposes?

And is it not strange that thou knowest about and have been told about another one of the unseen forces which will likewise perform for thee, and yet thou chooseth to go about thy daily affairs without it, preferring in its stead the flickering, unsure light of man-made candles?

Reflections

_____

_____

_____

_____

_____

_____

_____

_____

_____

_____

_____

_____

_____

_____

_____

_____

_____

_____

_____

_____

My Friend, Consider The Thief

My friend, consider the thief.

"Damnation and all the curses of God... my goods have been taken from me in the stillness of the night! Call the guard... the prosecutor... alert the jailer... I will have justice!"

My friend, perhaps unknown to thee, and, possibly, far from thine understanding, thou art seeing justice enacted, for nothing happeneth to thee by chance.

"But as a child, I learned the error of theft, for I stole a trinket from the shopkeeper and was forced to return it, and from that day to this, I swear, I have never again taken that which belongs to another."

Splendid, my friend, and wise were the ones who guided thee, and there is no doubt that thy word is true, but that does not change what is. For thou hast walked the earth before... in a day which thou canst not recall, and yet, which thy soul has record of. And if thou art pure from childhood, then thy wrongdoing cometh from another time and all that transpires now is but the outcome of that which happened before.

"Impossible! Foolishness! Be gone, talebearer of nonsense!"

My friend, it is but the truth that thou art sending away. But before leaving thee, let the truth tell thee one more time; thou reapest what thou hast sown, for that is the law, and if thou dost not break the chain of that which thee thyself hast established, thou shalt continue to reap until understanding dawneth within thee.

And if it will help thine understanding, recall the question that was asked centuries ago... Lord, why was this man born blind... because of his own sins or the sins of his parents?

"Wait, if this is true..."

It is true.

"Then how do I break the chain of my own wrongdoing?"

Thou knowest the way.

"I?"

The way and the truth and the life are within thee, and thou hast a thousand times recited the law that severeth the chain.

"I?"

My friend, has it been naught but mumbling to thee, dost thou truly not understand that as thou forgiveth, thou shalt be forgiven?

Reflections

MY FRIEND CONSIDER

My Friend,
Consider Creation

My friend, consider creation. Ah, thou canst see the rainbow arched above thee across the sky, and thou canst follow the colours as they meld together and divide in perfect harmony, and thou canst make dye from the growing things of the earth, and thou canst arrange these hues upon thy drawing tablet to resemble the pattern of the rainbow, and thou canst lean back and say, "Ah, I have created a work of art," and indeed, my friend, thou hast created a work of art.

And thou knowest in thy heart that all of that which is—has been created, and thou dost not often question that it was God who first brought forth the rainbow which thou dost imitate, and it was God who first brought forth the living things of the earth from which thou makest the colours of thy palette. No, my friend, thou dost not often question, for this seems reasonable to thee.

Perhaps, however, there is something which thou art unaware of, and perhaps, the hearing of it will tickle thine ears, but nonetheless, this is true. It appears that thou art even greater than thy God, for though it seems that all things were created by him, thou hast created that which thy God can not.

Thou hast taken the colours like unto all the portions of the earth... the browns and golds and ambers of soil, the pale yellows of wheat, the lightness of warm sand, the dark shades of stones behind the waterfall which give to the water its shimmer of life, the bronze and tawney rusts of rocky cliffs, yes, thou hast taken the colours of brown and gold and amber, of pale yellow, of tan and white, the colours of ebony and bronze and tawny rust, and thou hast 'created' a pattern of confusion and dis-harmony, of rancor and chaos which mystifies thy God and causes him to weep, for these are the rich and warm hues which he appointed unto the forms of his beloved children.

Reflections

_____

_____

_____

_____

_____

_____

_____

_____

_____

_____

_____

_____

_____

_____

_____

_____

_____

_____

_____

_____

_____

_____

My Friend, Consider The Wind

My friend, consider the wind. Thou dost strut upon the earth quite swelled with thine own self, and over and over thou dost declare,,. "Show me!" Thou dost converse and thou dost exhort and thou sayest, "I can see no God... there is no God." And thy words drift away on the winds which also thou canst not see.

Wouldst thou say, "I can see no heart within my body... there is no heart." Or wouldst thou remove thy heart to satisfy thine own demand of "Show me!" Ah, my puzzled friend, know, that with each beat of thine own heart, trillions of hearts beat at the same moment as the great pulse of everlasting life permeates all the created.

Know, that with the sound, sturdy thump within thine own breast, there is the same beat... rhythmic, sure and true within those to the right of thee and those to the left of thee and within the eagle which soars upon the wind.

My friend, when thou canst grasp that certain truth of one in all and all in one, then thou shall gaze upon eternity, for indeed, heartbeat is one.

As surely as the morning comes, and thou knowest that morning cannot not come, thou shalt know that the pulse of life is love which floweth through all... that the pulse of life is wisdom which is stored in vast untapped wells within thine own being and stored in smaller portions within the eagle who need not see the wind to soar thereon.

Perhaps, my friend, in the next beat of thine own heart, which indeed, thou canst not see, understanding will dawn in thy soul and transport thee to heights unknown, where, as the eagle, thou canst view that vast panorama beneath thee, and declare, "Ah, it is as I knew it was from the beginning," for thou shalt know the wind to be.

Reflections

MY FRIEND CONSIDER

My Friend, Consider Loneliness

My friend, consider loneliness. Thou dost surely know that the everness of love swirls eternally, like a gentle breeze... above, below, and around and in all. What hast thou taken for thy portion, and what hast thou given of thy portion, or hast thou chosen another way?

Hast thou taken loneliness for thy companion while the bud of the rose at thy window beckons thee to behold its beauty and to watch it unfold into its own magnificence. Would that the bud could speak to thee and say, "Be thou like me, my friend, for I am beauty, and I am joy. I am content to be part of. I give to all who pass by, give everything that I am, and they take of me and it increases their happiness. And when my day is over, I shall not be sad, for when the time is come again, I shall 'be' again, and I shall strive to be more beautiful than I am.

Be thou not lonely, for behold, only a small portion of 'that which is' has been allotted to me... oh... would that I had feet to carry myself to the dark and dreary places of the earth... would that I had hands to place myself in a bowl and bring joy to a saddened one... would that I could take the seed of myself and send me to distant shores for those who have never seen such as I.

Ah, yes, my friend, consider thine own portion of 'that which is', for thou canst do these things. If thou wouldst care to, cut me from this vine and take me to one you know. I will be a bond between you. I will give you my perfume, my brilliance of subtle colour and my exquisite texture. I will fill the space where you are with all that I am and I will plant my seed of love between you, and it shall grow, and thy loneliness will be no more. I would like that, for then I could be more than I am.

And remember this, my friend, if it happens

that l am not at thy window, thou hast the oven in which to bake a loaf from the wheat of the fields. This loaf you could take to one you know, and then, you see, the wheat can be as l. Oh, my beloved friend, how l wish that 'to know' was another of the portions allotted to me, for there is a secret among all the living things of the earth, and l know not what it is. But somehow... someway... it seems... well... it's something like the never-ending gentle breeze which caresses me."

Reflections

_____

_____

_____

_____

_____

_____

_____

_____

_____

_____

_____

_____

_____

_____

_____

_____

_____

_____

_____

My Friend, Consider Someday

My friend, consider someday. Thou beholdest the man of many years, stooped and grey of beard. Thou dost hear him mutter what to thee is but foolishness, and thou sayest in thy heart, "Be gone from my path, old man, for I have no time for thee. I shall pamper thee a moment and nod in thy direction, but the world awaits me and I must not keep it in abeyance too long, for indeed, mine own journey through this earth is of the only importance."

How true, my friend, how very, very true... for there are things which thou must do. Thou must prove to those around thee thine own greatness, thine ability to amass the riches of the earth, to surpass thy neighbor in knowledge, in wisdom, and in wealth, for thou hast determined that this is the way of things.

And yet, my friend, in thine own heart there is a whisper from ages past which thou hast chosen to ignore, for to give heed would, of course, cause thee to keep the world in abeyance and would keep thine own greatness from being proved.

They are eleven words, my friend, words of the very simplest order, but since thou hast chosen not to know them, be assured that someday when thou art old and lonely, when thou art stooped and grey of beard, there will be those who will hear thee mutter what to them is foolishness, and they will say in their hearts, "Be gone from my path, old man, for I have no time for thee."

They shall pamper thee for a moment and nod in thy direction, but the world awaits them and they must not keep it in abeyance too long.

Reflections

MY FRIEND CONSIDER

My Friend, Consider Laughter

My friend, consider laughter. If in thy journey through the earth thou hast lived at all, thou surely hast known those moments when joy has bubbled up within thy being and caused thee to burst forth with joysound. And thou knowest that it is an... all by itself thing in thy life, and thou knowest it is a... me and thee thing, it is an... all of us thing.

And at times it can cause thy very body to ache. It makes thee to cry, "Life is beautiful, life is good and indeed, I am glad that I am." And without this mirth to break the pattern of life's greyness, at times, life would be quite dim.

Thou canst recall joysounds of thine own past and even now it causeth a smile to cross thy countenance, and this is as it should be, for it is true, that that which is—is.

But always, my friend, keep this one note tucked within thy heart—if thine own laughter causeth thy neighbor to weep, causeth him to shrink, causeth him to die a little—cease.

Reflections

_____

_____

_____

_____

_____

_____

_____

_____

_____

_____

_____

_____

_____

_____

_____

_____

_____

_____

_____

_____

_____

My Friend, Consider Riches

My friend, consider riches. Do not all the treasures of gold and silver, of diamonds, of silks, of rubies and sapphires lie yet in the tombs with the bones of those who clung to them, or in the hands of thieves who have walked the earth in ages past?

Consider, oh consider, my friend, what is that which thou shalt take with thee when thy shell is returned unto the earth? Only that which thou hast engraved upon the pages of thine own book. Are thy pages full of love and kindness, of joy and laughter? Pray that it is so, for it is from these pages that the soul draws its nourishment and builds its ever onward-going path.

What hast thou given thy soul to feast

upon? Surely, thou hast given thyself thy full portion of love and of kindness to give to those in the place where you are, and surely thou knowest that thy portion is unlimited, for always, goodness and mercy are at thy disposal.

My friend, if thou hast truly filled the pages of thy book with the greatest portion of love which thou couldst garner, then thou hast given thy soul that to which it is entitled. But perhaps, thou hast chosen to fill thy pages with other things, for indeed, thou art free to do so, and if thou wouldst rather, my friend, remember, it is thy privilege to build a tomb as large as a section of land and to store therein thine accumulation of stones.

Reflections

MY FRIEND CONSIDER

My Friend, Consider The Vineyard

My friend, consider the vineyard. What dost thou see? Behold, acres of sturdy plants... vines laden with the fruit of themselves... seest thou not the clusters in all their crowded glory waiting for the hand of man to sever them from their place and use them to his own pleasure... to grace his table with their infinite array of purple, green and azure hues... to crush them and partake of their golden nectar.

Dost thou see this, my friend, and dost thou know that the fruit of the vine cannot conceive of itself as anything but beauty and goodness? And if, for one moment, it glimpsed itself being used for the destruction of man, its friend, it would truly spend its time in sadness. For there is no way that it could 'cease to be'.

Be sure, my friend, that if it could, it would shed a silent teardrop and if it could, it would whisper to thee and say, "My beloved friend, take of me and rejoice for a short season... at thy wedding feast and at thy celebration and in communion with that which is holy. Take me in a single cup with thy meal that I may add to the well-being of thyself, for I am sweet or I am tart as thou wouldst have me.

"But I beg of thee, my friend, do not take of me to thine own abomination, for truly, I would rather 'not be' than to be too much with thee and cause thee to lay thyself upon the city streets and make thy bed of hard and rocky cobblestones and become prey to thieves and to sickness and to die there from loneliness."

Reflections

_____

_____

_____

_____

_____

_____

_____

_____

_____

_____

_____

_____

_____

_____

_____

_____

_____

_____

_____

_____

My Friend, Consider Sunshine

My friend, consider sunshine. Ah, but thou dost bask there in the warm sands. Thou art stretched out beside the water's edge partaking of the rays which do pour down upon thee from the sun. Thy body eases and thy mind lets the cares of thy life slip away for a short season. Indeed, my friend, in these moments all is exceedingly well with thee, for the sunshine renews thy body forces and warms thy troubled soul.

And there are many, besides thee, upon the sands, for truly the sun does for all that which it does for one.

Wait, my friend, what is this sudden tensing within thee? What dost thou so suddenly see? Thy neighbor? Surely it is of no import now... What is this thou art saying? "The hell with him."

My friend, my friend, what art thou doing? Why art thou gathering together thy small parcel of belongings? Leaving? My friend, what dost thou conceal in thy heart which causest thee to take thine own self from the warmth and joy of the sunshine?

Reflections

MY FRIEND CONSIDER

My Friend, Consider Time

My friend, consider time. Surely, thou dost know that thou hast uttered a great and unalterable truth, and that thou hast said it, not once, not twice, but hundreds of times. Recall, my friend, for hast thou not said, "I have no time."

But thou hast done a strange thing, indeed, for thou hast measured thy lifetimes into portions and thou callest these portions 'years'. Thou hast measured these portions into further portions which thou callest 'months', and these months thou hast divided into smaller portions which thou callest 'weeks', and these weeks into 'days', and thy days into 'hours', and thine hours into 'minutes', and minutes into 'seconds', and these seconds into 'fractions' and thou hast termed this apportioning—TIME.

And then, thou hast commenced to establish a mystifying pattern according to the portions which thou hast set forth. Thou callest these patterns by strange names, for thou sayest, "We must race against time, we must beat time, we must make time, we must waste time, we must use time, we must kill time, we must buy time, we must bide time, we will lose time, we will run out of time..."

Thou hast lined thy towers and thy hallways and thy pockets with devices which keep ever before thee this apportioning of life which thee and thee alone in all the universe hath established, and yet, strangely thou declarest always the truth, for thou sayest "We have no time."

And indeed, my friend, there is NO such thing as TIME.

Reflections

_____

_____

_____

_____

_____

_____

_____

_____

_____

_____

_____

_____

_____

_____

_____

_____

_____

_____

_____

_____

My Friend, Consider Judgment

My friend, consider judgment.

Thou art a man who has walked the earth many years and thou dost declare with justification... "I am a man of sound judgment, for I have much knowledge and wisdom to draw upon from these, mine years of experience."

Rememberest thou the time, my friend, when thou didst see thy neighbor walk unsteadily from the back portion of his house to the barn which lay some distance away and thou sayest to thyself, "Aha, mine neighbor has tipped the cup of joy too heavily, but so be it." And lo, the following day, thou didst see the same as the day before and thou didst say to thyself, "Aha, again."

And day followed day, and with each day thou didst see the same neighbor stumble and totter to the outmost building to tend the animals therein. The time came when thou didst keep thy mutterings no longer to thyself, for thou didst whisper to thy neighbor on the other side and say, "Our neighbor does indeed too much partake of the cup of joy, for each day l behold him as he staggers from place to place." And thy neighbor on the other side joined thee and said, "Aha, so too l have beheld him."

Thou didst establish a fact between thee, and between thee, thou and this other neighbor poured out many whispers to those around, until many did see and observe with thee the actions of thy neighbor who stumbled and faltered. One day thy tottering neighbor fell ill and soon afterwards his heart ceased to beat, and his shell was placed in a box and set in the earth and covered with dirt.

Thee and all thy neighbors gathered about in thy cloaks of mourning and thou didst look sadness into each other's eyes and thou didst even then whisper, "Too many cups of joy."

What thee and all those standing with thee did not know was this—there is an infirmity within the body of a man which causeth him to totter and stagger and stumble much in the manner of one who has had too many cups of joy. And what else thee and those with thee did not know was this—that thy neighbor in the ground had not once tipped a cup of joy to his lips... no... not even at his own wedding feast.

So, my friend, if thou considerest thyself a man of sound judgment, follow first that which was so clearly given... judge not.

Reflections

_____

_____

_____

_____

_____

_____

_____

_____

_____

_____

_____

_____

_____

_____

_____

_____

_____

_____

_____

_____

My Friend, Consider Tomorrow

My friend, consider tomorrow.

Thou knowest this much... tomorrow will come. Thy men of science, with their many tools, say to thee, "The sky shall thus and thus... the rays of the sun shall so this and so that," and in this manner, my friend, thou canst prepare thyself for certain of the elements; but be ever certain that these, thy great men of science do not establish the thus and so of the elements, for the elements proceed quite upon their own in patterns of the cosmos which to thee and thy great men, shall always be unfathomable.

But, my friend, what of thine own tomorrow? Art thou sending fear and worry and turmoil ahead to hover over thee as the darkest of clouds and the strongest of winds? Dost thou desire the roaring of thunder and the torrents of rain? Surely, thou wouldst rather have the warmth of the solar rays and the smile which it brings to thine own countenance and to that of thy neighbor.

Be certain, my friend, that the cosmos follows patterns of its own, and brings to tomorrow that which it will. Be equally certain that in thine own ongoing, thou dost much the same.

Reflections

MY FRIEND CONSIDER

The promised preview of the upcoming book MY FRIEND, CONSIDER THAT WHICH IS awaits you. These early words offer a first step into the next part of your journey, encouraging you to continue forward with an open mind and a receptive heart. Within these few pages, you will glimpse the tone, the teachings, and the long-forgotten truths that will be explored more fully in the complete volume. Our hope is that this brief preview will spark your interest and prepare you for all that is yet to come when the full work is released in 2026.

My Friend, Consider
THAT WHICH IS
By Dru Ann Kenner

Truly, picture the ocean island—the palm trees swaying in ever same rhythm, warm sun, lilting music, children running the beach, laughter vibing the air—ah, paradise. This is the little island, the one off by itself, many hundreds of miles from the big one with the grand hotels and the airports and the partying. That too is an island, but it is from the small island that we form our picture; for, though palm trees sway on both, they are indeed vastly different.

Men the world over seek the islands of the ocean. They fly the world's largest planes, sail the ocean's grandest ships, and in due time reach their destination. They fill the hotels and the eating places, and for a while, the amusements hold them in a certain spell, for they are experiencing that "something different," and their days are filled with excitement and activity, and they seek to do all that there is to do.

They gather together expounding upon the beauties of the island, the ocean, the peoples, the customs, the progress and then at some later day, to themselves in a time of quiet reflection, or in a moment of conversational truth, they say, "I have been to the islands and it is not there—what I long for is not in the islands of this world."

No man is an island? Indeed. Every man is two islands; that larger one of his own activity with its many, many happenings, and the smaller one of quiet music, of laughter on the beach, and communion with the stars. Sometimes, sadly, he never finds his own "little" island.

Perhaps it could be best pointed out in this manner: once there were three little children, all born much at the same time. They were very close companions and shared all moments of the day, then strangely, one of them ceased to grow. He did not cease to be, he did not regress, he simply ceased to grow. For a while, the other two kept looking back, but then their lives became very active and full. They grew on into manhood and, looking back, became less and less frequent, for, of course, the living of life is a most time and energy-consuming process. But even so, they could never quite forget the third child; there were always reminders along the way, coincidences and random thoughts. No, they could never quite forget; there would always be that touch of sadness, the incompleteness, the wondering.

If the three children are likened to the three aspects of one's own self, it could be stated thusly. The first child—the body with all its inherent potential of growth; the second child—the mind with its great potential to learn and absorb; the third child—the spirit, equally with its potential for growth and expansion. Body, mind, and spirit, and for a season they grow in balance; for what is termed "the innocence of babyhood" is but the ongoing, self-generating power of the soul, inherent within each newborn just as body growth is inherent within the cellular structure.

Beautiful! The body is fed, and it grows. The mind is taught, and it develops. The spirit? Aha, sometimes it is guided, sometimes not. It has propelled itself up to a point—it must equally have nourishment and guidance, or it will flounder and grow at a much slower pace, and if it is totally ignored, it will eventually forget most of that which it knows, that which it brought with it into the infant.

One of the most ridiculous statements which Christ ever made while talking to a group of full-grown men was this, "Except that ye become as little children, ye shall no wise enter the kingdom of heaven." Can a grown man in all his worldly wisdom become as a little child? We think not and yet, there is this meaning which we know to be true—that unless a man stops at some point in his journey through the earth and reaches back for that third child, that area of himself which he brought with him, that surge of trusting, knowing innocence, and unless he gives it nourishment and opportunity to grow to the dimension of his body-self and of his mind-self, then he shall never cease his searching for the little island which he so desperately yearns for. And, if he finishes this cycle on the earth without reaching back, he will, during his last days, look around him sadly and say, "Something's missing."

Be assured that Christ knew what he was talking about, that he knew for a man to reach back into his life for that part of himself which had been stifled and had ceased to grow in proportionate balance to the rest of himself, was to expand the dimension of the full-grown man into greater joy, greater accomplishment, and greater love. For the full grown man had accumulated his cache of belongings, his entourage, his knowledge, but to add the child who beholds all of nature as wondrous—each morning a delight—who trusts in the very nature of his own being and those around him, who absorbs love and gives love, who laughs and runs with the wind and knows beyond all doubt that life is GOOD . . . it is this part of man's own nature that must be recaptured, fed and guided.

Impossible.

Is it impossible for a man to laugh at a comic happening while he is in the midst of deepest sorrow? Not at all, for that which is—is.

Ah, how men fool themselves. They leave the third child behind, and between their mind and their body, they establish a mode of living based on "goodness". This is as great a folly as to think oneself smart because he grasps the concept of two plus two equaling four, for being good implies not being bad, and by what standards does a man determine his own goodness? By his own standards, of course, and these can be as varied as the stars.

Good men have wrought untold destruction on the face of earth for eons passed, for always a man will determine the basis of his own goodness.

No, it is not enough to determine within oneself what is good. One must know, must acknowledge, must recognize and must set upon an established law of HIS being in the same manner as he acknowledges, recognizes and acts upon the established law of planetary being—the Law of Gravity. No man fears that his own physical being shall, by some quirk, be released from the earth's gravitational law and set adrift in the cosmos.

For all operational spheres of existence, whether they be visible or invisible, there are established laws that govern the operation of each. The laws of man – a composite of soul and body are as clear, as exact and irrevocable as the Law of Gravity is to the planetary being of earth.

The SUPREME LAW is that which governs the operational sphere of MAN. It was given in commands, for man had long missed the point. You shall love your God with all your mind and all your body and all your soul, and you shall love your neighbor and you shall love your own self. Bear in mind, these are NOT suggestions. The "do" commandments include the total teachings of ALL the masters of ALL religions and will be found worded in one manner or another in all religions, but nowhere except through Christ as a command. The import of ALL his authority lies inherent within this statement, and again—it was not a SUGGESTION!

If he had not known that it was the SUPREME LAW of life, he would not have established it as a NEW commandment, new, being that which was NOT until that moment.

To comply with this law by bits and snatches is the method by which a good man establishes his own goodness, and then he further deludes himself by rigorously living up to these standards.

Let us take a close look at a very "good" man...

✧

For those who wish to continue with *My Friend, Consider That Which Is*, you may request notification of its release by emailing MyFriendConsider@gmail.com with "That Which Is" as the subject line. A limited number of complimentary advance copies will be offered to the first 100 readers when the book is ready.

✧